Love

FROM A WORKING CLASS HEART

PHIL NEND

Matador
5 Weir Road
Kibworth Beauchamp
Leicester LE8 0LQ, UK
Tel: (+44) 116 279 2299
Fax: (+44) 116 279 2277
Email: books@troubador.co.uk
Web: www.troubador.co.uk/matador

ISBN 978 1848763 494

British Library Cataloguing in Publication Data.
A catalogue record for this book is available from the British Library.

Typeset in 11pt Book Antiqua by Troubador Publishing Ltd, Leicester, UK

Matador is an imprint of Troubador Publishing Ltd

You can close your eyes to things you don't want to see, but you can't close your heart to things you don't want to feel...

Author Unknown

For Mum, Stuart & Andrea, my niece Charlotte

PREFACE

There are all different kinds of Love, the way you love your partner, wife/husband, how you love your children to how you love your parents or friends. Feelings of guilt are another emotion and the sadness you feel with someone you love dies. Also, the feeling you have when someone you love takes their love away.

None of my poetry has titles – as that will be up to you, the reader of my book, to give it their own title, as it will be your imagination visualising the words, and relating to your own experience of a feeling we cannot hide or buy. As, at times, we can't express or say how we feel to our loved ones until sometimes it's too late.

Everyone falls in love at some stage or other in their life. No matter who you are, your religious background or even beliefs.

Searching high and low
I knew I would find you
My heart told me so
A rose from my heart
Sent to you your smile
Shining in full view
No man of lies
This angel before my eyes
Feeling so right, leading
The way through brilliant light
Now let the love begin as minds entwine
Our hearts sharing same goals
To bring comfort to our lives
Together blow away rainy clouds
Watch as they disperse like busy crowds
Your loving touch feels so right
So peaceful now will I sleep tonight
Holding each other in our hearts
From this day forward
We shall never be apart.

Our journey of life is clearly mapped out
Which path you take my love
Is nothing but fate?
I have been following a shining star
Not from my sight but from my heart
As I looked in the sky there was none
My spirit guide told me fear not my son
For your soul will guide you
To the star you seek
Follow your heart be strong not weak
For she will be waiting so beautiful and fair
Piercing green eyes flowing silken hair
The warmth of her love
Will not be hard to find
So there is no need to feel
Empty weak or blind.

*S*un shining through a lonely heartache
Waiting loves harbour
Within heavens theatre
Just me and my shadow
Searching tomorrow's dreams
Is this what life has to offer?
Maybe this is not all it seems
Mirror inside of you
Reflects outside of me
Just take time
Time all that's needed
Please await patience
Before your very eyes
As witnesses to love two hearts bonding
So strong together alone
In paradise do we belong,
Or chase our hopes all day all night long,
Walking though a minefield of feeling,
Just for someone so special
My love is more than just meaning.

*T*he doors of my past firmly shut behind
I know I need the love that so gentle and kind
I look to the moon in clear night sky
The stars sparkling so bright
Showing me the path
One step at a time
I know I must go
As I take each step
The stronger I become,
I hear your voice
Makes my spirit dance
My heart and soul glow
For the strength you have given
Has kept me from harm
Your love your laughter
Kindness and charm
My path so clear now
You stand there before me
The angels take a bow
Let your soul entwine with my heart
From this day may we never be apart.

*I*n my sleep last night I dreamt
An angel came to me
So familiar did she look
Then whispered in my mind
The love you await is
There before your eyes
Woken to sunshine clearest blue skies
In my thoughts what the angel said
Where was this love to find?
Vision came to me in such very short stride
Heartfelt feeling so strong
This love just could not hide
My angel standing there with emerald green eyes
Took my heart so gently cradled in her soul
Filled my mind with love not fear
Took me to the highest mountain
Shared her love with me
Look out to the world
It's there for us to be
Our lives now together
Herein till eternity.

The lessons of our past
Make us who we are tomorrow
Love, laughter, joy, hurt and sorrow
Spirit guide will see us through
The pain clouded memories tears of rain
Take our hand bathe us in divine light
Cleanse our soul to hold us in vein
Do not worry of yesteryear
Negative thoughts and grudges to bear
We cannot change the past its set in stone
Take a step forward to our heavenly home
Embracing each day with the journey that comes
My love will protect you
A heart shaped dome a cloak
I shall put around you strong as oak
Light as silk my spirit soul and love
Shall never be lost
I now have the love I will never lose
Let our future take its course
A path the angels love will choose.

The stormy clouds on their way
Sunshine breaks a brighter day
Insecurities broken heart
No more new path before me
Strength to open the door
You have gave me wisdom and tools
Courage to jump from the ship of fools
Is it fate as I look to the skies?
My soul mate before me
Wiping tears from weary eyes
Spirit enlightened
Soul no longer timid or frightened
Heart alive with love you give
Like a rose blossoming when spring arrives
My destiny graces before me
Struck in awe my love
Reaching your hearts shores
My aura in your command
Leading the way hand in hand
Together we will be in eternal bliss
From that very first soft gentle kiss
Guardian angels standing proud
Cherubs singing out aloud
Forget I not this magical day
I've found the love that has awoken
Never again shall my spirit
Be low or heart is broken.

We are the architects of life
Take advice from the young at heart
Let our spirits entwine with our soul
Join as one so never apart
Feel the love I give
Float to your dreams
Like sunshine on a new summer's day
Rays bursting through cloud seams
Listen to angels embrace sing dance
Laying a path of hope step by step
Hand in hand we will find utopia
With skies that shine in your eyes
Sun that beats in rhythm with my heart
No tears of rain fears or pain
Birds of paradise sing in trees
Our bodies catch gentle warm breeze
Await the starlit night sky full moon shining
Stars gleam like diamonds
Take the magic never let go
I will be by your side won't let you fall
Feel my soul you will only have to call into the heavens
When you awake from this beautiful dream
Refresh your mind all will come back
My love soul and spirit
Won't be hard to find.

We don't know where our future lies
We know where our past has been
Together be strong
Let us walk into the unknown
My heart in your hands
Cries with a gentle sigh
Your love I know will protect
Let us open the way forward
No need to tread on egg shells
Put our trust in each other
Feel love's strength
Our wisdom gets stronger and stronger
Your love picks me up
Are you my soul mate I've been searching for?
Tell me it's true you lift my spirit
I feel your lips tingle as we kiss
You whisper my thoughts
Is this the match made in heaven?
All my life I've longed for
I can only make one promise
I will never stop loving you
Until the seas run dry
Let me fill your life with happiness
May you keep my final breath for eternity?
When I'm no longer here on this earthly plain
I will switch a light on in heaven for you
Forever from that day our love will go and on.

When I look at you
The sun shines through my soul
My heart misses a beat
You embrace my dreams
To see such beauty
With an adorable smile
Could I not ask for any more?
But only to be with you
For a cuddle and a kiss
Feel the warmth of your love
Your eyes meet mine
Searching our dreams
Looking for paradise
Our minds entwine
To hold you for a second
That could last an eternity
Where time stands still
While you hold my spirit
My soul my will.

*W*hen you look into my eyes
Tell me what you see
Do you see a past of sadness?
Do you see my soul?
Flickering like a candle in the wind
It is only when I feel your touch
My world lights up again
Lying with you in amazing daisy strewn fields
Views of a tranquil blue sea
Waiting for golden sunset
The stars to shine
Glittering in the moonlit sky
Staring up into the heavens
Watching angels gliding by
Sweet music you hear is not from celestial harps
But the love you have replaced
The music from my heart.

Whenever you're down
Remember this, I'll be your clown
Your eyes shine so bright
Your smile lights a million stars in the sky
I've fallen for this smile
Only my heart knows why
Let me take you by the hand
Past the stars to some heavenly land
Where seas are calm skies are blue
Palm trees sway in gentle breeze
Bright sun raises the birds sing for you
Before night falls stars come out to shine
Have no fears or worries
Your slender soft hands
Will be held firm in mine.

Whilst I lie here staring at the stars
My thoughts of you forever in my heart
Time standing still moon shining so bright
Door of my past closed firmly behind me
Future giving me courage and will
I wait to hear your voice
A voice that makes my heart skip a beat
Gives me butterflies
I know its not long before we meet
Early days I know
Step by step we'll go
Not too fast and neither too slow.

*T*ake my hand there is
Something I need to show you
Walk through the garden of my soul
It is here you will find heavens beauty
Rose's orchids of spectacular kind
They blossom for you as you will find
Please take one put it close to your heart
Hear angels playing their harps
I've found my soul mate you know it too
Our future waits for us to walk through
Not bound by emotional chains
Heavy hearts no longer in pain
My love I will lay before your eyes
Open your heart to my blue skies
When the day comes my soul departs
My love will be forever within
As you hold that flower
Close to your heart.

Something for you as your close to my heart
A special love that shall never part
Minds joined as one time stood still
Let the future begin free our will
I can give you nothing but my undying love
Witnessed by the angels above
Tomorrow will be another day
Yet let nothing at all stand in our way
Ups and downs life will be
This path was made for you and me
Arms open wide to shelter you from harm
My soul will cloak around you
To keep you warm
Look to the rainbow sunset
Just like the first time our eyes met
Every day my love grows stronger
For you bring your joys sorrows laughter too
Our judgement shall not cloud
Let us together stand so proud
My heart before you
Let it take a bow
From this day to eternity
My love for you will never let go.

Listen to my dreams with me
Dream a dream
What you see will be
Keep secrets locked in our hearts
Fun, laughter, sadness, two soul's desires
Only the two of us know
By day by night does my love glow?
There are no rules to our game
No need to hold dreams in shame
Break down the walls of my thoughts
Through a fountain of tears
Can you feel my fears?
Throw them into life's embers
Ready for a new beginning
No more secrets no more closed doors
Take my dreams together
Will shall share yours.

*T*ake a journey to the abyss of my heart
You will not get lost
Every turn every bend
Will lead you to the very end
Here you will find what you have been looking for
As you have the key to my heart's door
Should you not open?
You will never know what lies within my soul
Does not fear take the chance my love?
Will be there to embrace yours forever
You will always have a part of me
With you wherever you go
Whatever you choose to do
To absorb your tears of sadness
Bring you laughter and joy
As you will have released the man
No longer a boy

Here let me take you by the hand
Stand on the edge of the shore
Watch as the tides of time stand still
Sun sets await full moon to rise
Stars begin to dance with nightfall
Let evening breeze
Wrap itself around you
Give comfort through and through
Look out feel all the things you can see
No magic here just you and me
Listen to the gentle waves singing
Throw your fears into the darkness
You will not fall let go your free will
It will take you, no need to turn around
I'm there next to you
My love you can hold
As long as you wish
Take any path you chose
Two lots of love combined
You cannot lose
Feel the strength your love has now sewn
Let your eyes listen to the life ahead
No need to worry of nightmares and dread
I will be there next to you
Each step you tread.

I pick a star out of the night sky for you
To keep close to your heart
For the things you do
A ray of sunshine
You have brought into my life
No longer a stranger to myself
No longer afraid of shadows
My heart like a hot coal with loving glow
You took me under your wing
An angel are you
To the heavens does your spirit sing
Please let me take you on life's journey
Share, laughter, tears, sorrow
Awake to find a brand new dawn a new tomorrow
Breathe in the air so fresh
Cleanse your soul in golden sunshine
I ask will your love ever be mine?
Holding each other close
Withholding the sands of time.

Thank you for sharing with me
The sunshine in your heart
I feel your magical touch
Every time our eyes meet
I cherish every moment
We spend together
My love sent to you
It's now or never
Let us be free like songbirds
Singing our love
In the heavens orchards
Angels dance blossoms flowered
Watch our youth grow again
Before our eyes no more pain
No more goodbyes
A life time we shall spend
Not as only as lovers but as best friends
To carry for eternity
I was sent to you
You were sent to me.

I want you to know why I love you
You've brought me sunshine
That was not there, healed my soul
Took my worries away without any cares
Without you I wouldn't feel alive
If you weren't here by my side
Give me the strength
Close my past with pride
I want you to share a million wishes with you
But none shall be bigger than my heart
To shout at the top of the highest mountain
I love you
For us both to drink out of the fountain of life
Walk together through the gardens of the heavens
For you have given me the will to be me again
I shall not walk in your shadow but next to you
When you fall I will be there to catch you
Be with you through life's storms
To be there as you awake
To see that first beautiful smile on your face
I could give you a thousand reasons more too
But I love you most of all because your you.

*J*ust a quick word to say I'm thinking of you
Your skies forever blue
May your soul and spirit guide you with grace?
In whatever you do
You lift my day in every way
Even when things aren't going right
I have something to hold onto tight
So this is sent just for you
You're in my hearts thoughts
Through and through.

Would you join me in a duet my love
Make sweet music to the angels
Together we could watch them sing and dance
Our hearts too move in harmony
Let our minds wander in a breeze of beauty
Never letting go
We could light the dark skies
Watch the stars glittering off the silvery moon
Our hearts entwine into one
Touching every sense as we go along
Gently, slow, fast, together be as one
Hands held firm in each other's
With not a care in the world
Watch in wonder as
The night bows before us.

*Y*our love is a magnet to my heart
Sit and day dream whilst we're apart
Walking with you hand in hand
Through pastures green
Golden sunshine mystic woodlands
Never letting go of that feeling
Hearts as one
Fresh summer's morning
You give me butterflies deep inside
That wonderful excitement
You have my song in your heart
Only you can add sweet music to
Play in time knowing your love
Will be forever mine.

A midsummer's night gazing out
The bright full moon
My love can't wait for you
I know it be soon to see the stars
Reflecting off your eyes
Look into my smile
There hides no lies
To see the look upon your face
No clouds of judgement no not a trace
For you have taken my love
Together we dance from the heavens above
Hearts beat in time
Soul and spirit not out of line
The love you have given
Will be treasured in my heart
Do not worry we shall never part
Should my soul leave my body?
Do not shed tears
The love will be stronger than the start
I will build a home in our spiritual land
Walk you through gardens of beauty
Blue seas golden sands
Please I beg save your love
Eternal life, happiness and hope
Not far way for you and me
Whisper to the gods set your soul free
While the angels await with happiness and glee.

Nightfall's our dreams in touching distance
Dreams you have always wished
Never let go always hold on
Life comes life goes
Good times, bad, indifferent
The good that never far behind
But never let go of your dreams
For as long as the sun shines
Stars glitter off full moon
Your dreams will be there with you
Let fairies dance angels play
Birds sing listen to the trumpets
Echo from the minaret's in full glory
Embrace them like a mother
Holding her new born child
Let tomorrow be a new day
Embrace your dreams
Hold on don't let go
For in time they will
Be there before you.

A new dawn begins a new tomorrow
Blessed by an angel in my dreams
Sun shining through my mind
New life for me to find
Search neither high nor low
Standing before me this beauty
My soul takes a bow
You give me life when you take my hand
I stand in awe as my eyes do not lie
Passion ignited like fire from the heavens
We both can't deny love we have finally found
Spirit guides whisper not a sound
Approve do our heavenly beings
Smiling with grace
They know what our love means,
My heart was lost, yours was found
On a star we shall ride
Through the universe together we go
Into the unknown maybe
Lift each other with love not blindness
Light this path of sheer darkness,
Time stands still I will not let go
To your soul I've made the vow
Never in time shall it be broken
For my love you have awoken
Never again my heart be torn
Apart as my life rests in your soul
Together we stand and will not fall.

An angel saved my spirit and soul
Your heart I will heal with my love
Took me by the hand
To show me a glimpse of heavens above
Ties here your past of hurt shall be healed
Strength to you shall come back
You will walk again in golden fields
Your past will make you stronger
Just as the days get lighter
For I will not faulter by your side
My love is there for you
As your heavenly guide
Tears of sadness wiped away
Live for tomorrow not just today
Take the first step and bury your tears
I'm by your side do not have any fears
Do not be ashamed of whets happened in the past
A bright future awaits you at long last
Your time has not yet come
To join me in the heavens above
Live your life now and to the full
I promise you it shall never be dull
Take life as it is ups and downs
For your soul spirit and love
Will be protected with my angelic silken gown.

As dusk meets the night
tell me my love what would you want?
Would you want me to run you a hot bath?
Scented bubbles, rose petals scattered atop
Would you want me to help you?
Relax, a soothing massage
A glass of the finest wine
Maybe to take the strains away
Let us whisper our deepest thoughts secrets
To one another
Would you let me cradle you in my arms?
Let me watch over you while sleep
I'd stay awake just to hear you breathe
Gently wiping your hair from your brow
Keeping you from harm
Waiting for dawn to break morning
Dew glittering on the grass
When you awake that smile on your lips
A picture of sheer beauty
I thank the angels in the heavens
You're here with me.

As soon as I saw you,
I knew you were the one
When you smiled into my eyes
All insecurities had gone
For when I looked back
My hear knew what it meant
Nothing but sheer beauty
From heaven were you sent?
I'm no man of riches
Nor a man of lies
Only strength and courage
With this I know I'll get by
What I do have to give you
Is more than anyone could give?
I want you to realise
That my deep heartfelt love
My soul spirit
Without this I'd have no urge to live
One day I hope we'll be waiting
Hand in hand golden beach
Tree swept forest
Or some beautiful land
Somewhere I can whisper
Into your dreams
For now my spirit is with you
Fears are no longer what they seem.

un sets down, stars begin to shine
You can throw your worries away with mine
Let time stand still feel the warm night air breeze
Place your gentle hand in my palm
Now you feel at ease
So peaceful and calm
My spirit will lift you
My love I will borrow
Use your mind to reach out and see
A glowing light
There I am an angel that me
Use my strength
Watch your sorrows flee
Make your wish then sign your kiss
Keep them in a safe place
With your hopes and dreams
Should you ever lose them don't fall apart
Just whisper my name
Because they will be there in my heart.

*W*aterfall meets the rivers of your dreams
I look to your smile and the joy that it brings
Your voice comes to me like gentle breeze
Singing through the treetops
Turning tears to crystal raindrops
Making magical auras lighting night sky
My soul wants to shout to the world
This is not the end but the beginning
Waving the past a joyous bye
Jumping from the ship of fools
You have given me strength and spiritual tools
To build my life makes a new me
Like an undiscovered ocean, river or sea
Thank you for the gift you give
Now moving on with the will to live
Sadness and sorrow not in my tomorrow
My love will be there for you to borrow
Fear no longer to be afraid
Gods before me
With this new path I've made.

Before you came back into my life
My soul was scattered heart torn and shattered
Released liked into the wild
Your love has saved me from darkness
Your spirit has shown me the way forward
With heartfelt passion
Blind no longer
But desire and hunger
Ghosts of my past
Now blown into the wind
Such power does your love bring
Let me take a star from the sky
Place it your hands to thank you in abundance
Forever grateful for the love you give
My heart with open arms is all I can offer
Please take it for I'm no more worthy than a pauper
This love you have shown
I'm no longer alone
And pray you will be with me
For an eternity
A life we can build in
Love harmonic tranquillity.

I see your sadness feel your pain of tears
My heart aches too
Our love is nothing but in the lap of the gods
Patience not fear is all I ask
Search the emptiness within my soul
Two lives not yet complete
That day will come to us I promise
Passion over frustration
Pure love no more anger
Time I hear you say, how much longer?
Look to the heavens lead in vein
Questions answered fears thrown away
A past of torment now put to rest
My wish granted no longer second best
Together hand in hand
Put each other first
Brand new chapter
Our creation to loves new verse.

*C*an I take you to my garden?
To plant a special seed
A seed of love and hope
Is just what my garden needs
Maybe choose a rose or beautiful sunflower
With the light of love you give
I'll sit and watch them tower
I will nurse them like small children
No harm shall come to any
I can see the picture in your mind
This garden grows with grace
That what you're loving has give
To me a special place
As sun sets down and night begins to fall
I await the birds to wake me
With their morning call
For they will fill my heart
With joy and grace
That my garden you've made
Such a special place.

Can you hear me calling?
Do you see my love?
Falling from the greatest of heights
I give you heavenly delights
Will you be there?
To catch these in your heart
Gently ascending
Like rose petals in the breeze
Each one blessed with love
Just for your dreams
Time starts to slow not by chance
Our love will grow
Gently take that first kiss
Nothing our eyes won't see or miss
Heart beat beats in harmony
Playing to angelic symphony
Before us watch and take a bow
Feel the grace our heavenly beings show
The stars reflecting off your eyes
As our love begins to waltz
Through the skies.

Do not look into the mirror of your past
I beg you to untie the chains
That holds you down
Let them go feel free
To do as you wish my love
Look to the blue skies
The pot of gold at the end of the rainbow
Do not feel anger or anguish
For I will stand next to you
I won't let you down
Let us both follow that path
To love and happiness
Let me help you put that sparkle
Into that beautiful smile
Those crystal green eyes
Take that first step into the unknown
Please do not surrender
And hold your hands up in despair
Take your sorrows and blow them into the wind
Keep your best kept memories
Locked inside you for a rainy day
Above all else remember
Tomorrow is not too far away.

Do not lose your past like tears in rain
I will be there for you
To hold your heart
Keep you warm
My love is there to see
Release us both set ourselves free
To make love to you like never before
Beneath stars and moon on silken floor
Feel the heat passion over and over
Let there be no time
No waiting for morning
An eternity we become one
Finally new dawn begins
Future now with us step by step
We leave our sadness
Now let our loves begin this happiness.

Heartache confusion to name but two
Is through the love I have for you
Let your soul make decision
Your spirit will guide you to incise precision,
My heart too is broken and torn
Together my love we shall share a new dawn
Angels will guide our love shall not hide
Your hand in mine my heart in yours
Let past go close the doors
Please come with me share delights
Watch stars dance crystal moon lit nights
Join as one leave our fears
No sadness or sorrow just laughter with tears
Don't give up hope on me and you
The end will be the beginning
A new future into view.

I ask you my love to take a deep breath
Take my heart feel truth in my eyes
I live in hope one day we will be together
We cannot hide our honesty for one another
Holding our love that shall not tear us apart
You give my soul shelter and strength
Day by day our past has gone set in stone
Tomorrow has yet to come
For we are but mortal our lives all but done
Let our spirits sing to the heavens
Join as one heart beat with heart beat
Bow before angels and comets
Together start a new journey hand in hand
Our love will be so strong
In our new found land
No tears of sadness shall we shed
But tears of joy by step by step
To be left alone under the stars
No fears in our burning hearts
That day shall come
Trust me my love
Our tomorrow will be our today
It will not be late in any way
For to think of each other
Every second of time
I will be yours and you will be mine.

$\mathcal{I}$ find my soul wandering alone
Searching for that loving sparkle
Is true I'm not on my own
For when I look around
I can see what I have found
A peacefulness of calm
That will do my soul no harm
Your spirit in open arms
Taking me inside your love
I will abide, untruthfulness I won't hide
Taking me to heights I could only dream
If the love I've found what will it mean
You have picked me up gave me love
Warmth and strength cleansed my soul
Gave my heart a will to live again
But more than not a shelter in your heart
From life's pressures, strains and pains.

I found the recipe of love
I didn't have to look too high or too low
Or to the heavens above
I only had to glance into your eyes
To take my soul to paradise
Ingredients mix as bodies touch
Our love will never starve
As there is so much to give
To share like an endless stars flare
Reaching out as far as time can see
I will be there as you are for me
No other shall no our secret
Kept in angels hearts guarded by spirit
I leave you now with this in mind
My love for you will never be hard to find
Should you need strength in times of hurt?
My heart will be open to you
For solace and comfort.

I give you the key to my heart
From this day shall we never part?
Hold my tears in vein
Take away tormented pain
You give me life, give me strength
Join me in a duet of love
Blessed by angels
From the heavens above
A special wish I have for you
Let our dreams, happiness come true
Wrap your gentle soul with mine
Together be a one lost in time
Dance amongst the stars, silvery moon
Should tomorrow come it will be too soon
Our tomorrow will be our yesterday
As my love grows stronger
For you in every way.

I have a dream to share with you
Would you hold my heart?
In one hand and my love in another
Share my life's ups and downs
Laughter joys tears
My heart aches for your touch
A gentle kiss
The feel of heat from your body against mine
Sharing our love in endless passion
Over and over again
Let the sunrise watch the night fall
My heart sings out will you answer its call
Let's go all the way without hesitation
Lay our love's foundation
You and I were meant be
The gods have made our paths
This we can both see
From now and forever
My heart will be with you
And yours forever will be with me.

I just wanted you to know
That in your darkest times
I will be there with you
No matter how low
Touch my heart
Feel the light grow
Darkness lifts a smile appears
Your heart listens
Your spirit begins to sing
Let the rivers of your mind
Flow to your dreams
It is then your soul begins to glow
For even if I am not around
Just whisper my name
I will be there
Arms reaching out love lay bare
Do not worry panic or fear
For I will never be far
But always so near.

I only have one heart to give, it's for you
Go on take it
I know it will be looked after
Never broken
Please though treat it with care
Will love you forever more
Give your soul a new lease of light
Nothing will ever come between us
Guardian angels will work in harmony
Keep us both from harm
Your intuition will not let you down
Share our dreams together
Carry each other through rainy days
Blow the grey clouds away
Watch blue skies appear
Now you have my heart
I see the bright future
Your love comes to me
Nearer and nearer.

I see the love echo in your eyes
You keep my heart
When we say goodbyes
No need to rush time
Now I know your mine
I will lift you so you can
Take the stars out from the skies
Our love will wrap around each other
To keep us both warm
All my life I have known
Waited for this moment
Never to let go
Forever will sun shine in our lives
Let me take you to the four corners of the universe
Together we will see it through
Should darkness ever fall upon you
Do not worry I will pick you up
As my heart has been there and back too.

*I*f I could ask you to dance
Would you join me?
Before the music of angels
Together holding each other's love
Skipping through stars
Touching the heavens above
As our hearts meet beating in time
I cannot begin to tell
What this means for you to be mine
Eyes staring deep into each others
My soul waiting to ignite the passion
Tip-toeing on the edge of time
Through the universe we go
No worries no cares we get to paradise
That we know my love
Reaching your love
Tell me how you feel
As before you my heart
Soul spirit shall kneel
Forever yours from this moment on
Let this new day begin let the old be gone
I'm so glad now I had the chance
To ask you my love
For your hearts last dance.

If I were a seed I'd be a seed of a great oak
As you plant me in your garden
You would watch me grow
With that growth comes also my love
For you my darling this would be an eternity
Just like the strength of this beautiful tree
Arms branching out holding both you and me
To protect us from harm
Hold you close when life is so calm
Your love for me would give me growth
My heart would sing I'd never be low
My soul would be there for you
On a dark winter's night
To keep you warm your spirit light
Whilst you lie in my arms
And give me that gentle kiss
A loving smile upon your lips
Our hearts take flight
Together we are one
Entwined in passion
As our love goes on and on.

If I were the words you would be the music
Together we would be one
Joined by heart soul and spirit
Do not fear worry or panic my love
Our journey together is not yet done
The difficulties we go through in this life
Made us who we are
Past in concrete future not too far
The earthly plane is mere but a test
The real journey starts when we are at rest
Together as one in our spiritual realm
Our ship will wait with us both at the helm
To take us across clear blue seas
Lands of beauty singing birds gentle swaying trees
Sun shining down this is our home
No hatred pain jealousy or disease
When time comes our hearts will be one
Both will know it shall be done
At heaven's gate I will await
For you my love it will never be too late
A gift for you my soul lay bare
Touch love with your gentle care
Our minds entwine with passion so bright
No fears or darkness
To see us through the night.

*I*f my heart were a star
You would see it shining in the night sky
Like a solitary diamond
When smoke clouds your mind
Look to the skies there
You will see my heart
For you to hold cradle
Nurture to keep you from harm's way
Glowing like a red hot coal
Do not fear my love
It will not be theft if you keep it
But a mere token of love
Strength, courage for you to hold everyday
My love will be with you shall never stray
Feel my smile shine through you
Enlighten your heavens
Let sun shine through your eyes
Angels open their arms to you
Watch and believe as your heart takes flight
Keep on sleepy dreaming
As my heart stays with you
If I could write a love story
It would be the happiest love story ever wrote
If I could sing you would hear
The most beautiful song ever sung
So keep this close to your heart
For eternity and a day
We shall never be apart.

In this life don't let your love linger
Don't stab my heart with a poisoned finger
I lay my love before you
Shower you with grace, passion
Show you the beauty of the heavens
From the finest views
Stand and watch as our souls
Wander into spiritual gardens
Lit by stars like a chandelier
See our ship finally come in
Long awaited now our hearts are singing
No longer alone a happiness of plenty
For an eternity to come
Love joined together
As we become one.

*L*et me take you by the hand
Stand on the edge of the shore
Watch as tides of time stand still
Sun sets await the full moon to rise
Stars begin to dance with night fall
Let the evening breeze wrap itself around you
To give comfort through and through
Look out feel all things you can see
No magic here just you and me
Listen to the gentle waves singing
Throw your fears into darkness
You will not fall let go
Let your free will take you
No need to turn around I'm there next to you
My love you can hold as long as you wish
Take any path you choose
Two lots of love combined
How can you lose?
Feel the strength your love has now sewn
Use your eyes, listen to the life ahead
No need to worry of nightmares and dread
For I will be next to you with each step you tread.

Let us stand together
Not looking into each other's eyes
But looking outward toward the stars and moon
Towards golden sunsets
Where we can be alone together just me and you
Our love will see it through
Never to be alone again
Never will our hearts be filled with rain
Feel life we give each other soul and spirit
Get younger and younger never older
Take each day with love and grace
Open new doors without haste
Stand in awe as mountains touch
Is this not a moment too soon to miss?
All I ask is one final wish
To give me that first loving, gentle kiss.

Listen with your heart
You will hear my footsteps coming to you
My love will not be far behind
Open the gates to your soul
Show me the view of your mind
Here I give you the rainbow in my hand
A kaleidoscope with multitude of colours
Beating in time with your heart
No longer looking for answers
They are there in my eyes
A new love a new start
Let others talk about us telling lies
Does this come as any surprise?
With all the love in the world to give
This life is for us to live
Ask only to be your true soul mate
As I kneel before your hearts gate.

My darkest times you are there to pick me up
In times of sadness and despair
You shower me with love everyday
Give me hope from heavens above
You heal past thoughts of hurt and pain
Your wisdom brings me sunshine not rain
When I sleep and dream of sweet things
I know your there cradling me in your wings
To keep me safe and out of harm's way
Give me strength to get through the day
So I thank you for all the love you give
And know we shall never be apart
As my spiritual home is in your heart
You give me courage, hope, vision and sight
I thank the gods in the heavens
For my angel of light.

My heart to you is an open door
Love within for ever more
My spirit will guide your slender soul
To be together our passion shall be sown
You pick me up, you give me hope
No longer walking life's tightrope
For shelter I have found in your wings
My angels send you their heavenly blessings
Together let us take this life
With laughter and happiness
No trouble or strife
I now know you are the one
My love I give to you
Like an undiscovered ocean
Feel my life through your fingers
Hearts as one there are no borders
You have given me a reason to live again
No more sadness trauma or pain.

My love feels so right
In your presence you're my daylight
That shines in my heart
Together let us skip through clouds
Hand in hand within blue skies
Not a care in the world, feel the highs
Show me your beauty within
Hold my love forever
I look into your eyes
I see the eighth wander
Take me to paradise
Past the heavens and back again
Watch as time stands still
Never look back through
Dark cloud or rain
Place our kisses in cupped hands
Blow them into our future
Make new found pastures
Doors opening for new adventures
Me and you together
Let our love get stronger
For here after not a day longer.

Never let the moment pass
To say goodbye
Never the let your heart
Keep asking why
Never let your tears run dry
Let go follow your soul
This love you have gave
Has made my heart whole
I give you all complete devotion
You have been there
To heal my emotion
I see this in your eyes reflection
My love is there for you
To take at night when you sleep
In morning when you awake
You're my guardian angel
Best friend, soul mate
Should I ever say I love you?
I know it would never be too late.

No more rain in my heavy heart
No more tears of sadness
No more denial, fears or madness
The secret is when I look into your eyes
I could never say a thousand goodbyes
My love is there for you to see
My soul felt your passion
You know it was meant to be
Lust at first sight cut through
A guilt edged knife
Loved like never before
Hypnotised as I needed more
Spellbound by such beauty
Our love for each holds no boundary
Released the fire within
Two hearts as one
Now let life begin
I could not ever love another
As I lay next to my spirits martyr
Stars angels come out to shine
I thank the gods in the heavens
You're next to me knowing your love
Will be forever mine.

Touch the moon, reach my smile
Touch the stars you will find my heart
I will lift you have no fear
Your dreams before you mile after mile
Is taking a chance taking a risk
Look within your divine
All your answers you will find
Love is strong never kind
Given the half chance
Could I take you for a midnight dance?
Together step by step
Through clouds of judgement
Overseas of heartache
Leave whispers on our shadows
Paradise in sight
Layer before us over golden lakes
Hold our spirits tight
Here our wildest dreams
Come into sight
Sapphire eyes reflecting off mine
A smile wrapped in my soul begins to shine
Now look back and tell me what you see
Clear blue skies gentle breeze
The future in full view
For you as you please.

Despair no longer
Time is all is needed,
Two hearts so close yet so far apart
Through mists of rain
Plant a seed of love
Feel my thoughts
Let them bow to your dreams
No more games
No more cat and mouse
Find the secret within me
Is it the answer your wish commands?
Live and let live
Begin tomorrow a new me, a new you
Past mistakes only borrowed
Watch them vanish
Real beauty lies within
Ignited long awaited passion
Do not look through my eyes
The secret lies within you
Open out like a flower in the spring
Watch as my heart will follow too.

Turn around see what's in front of you
A stream of sadness
Your dreams come true
A path of broken dreams
New life in full view
Is it there what you have been looking for?
My love will guide you through and through
It has been there for me now
Will be there for you
No need to look hard
Far and wide your happiness is all around
It will not hide
Clear your mind, feel your way
Tomorrow will bring sunshine
Not the rains of yesterday,
Forever will you be in my heart
You can see in my eyes
My love will never pass you by
Take heart from what i say
That happiness you seek
Not too far away.

My heart tells me you're the one
In my head the illusion is gone
Waiting for a sign
All I see the hands of time
Stuck in heaven's crossroads
Which step forward should I take?
The left the right maybe or turn back
To past mistakes teardrop falls
From the skies time to look around
Vision I see no more blinkered eyes
Strength within ignites with fire
First step forward passion desire
The goal I seek in full clear view
A new life found not for one but two
Join me step by step
When we reach our goal
My heart my soul
I will be there for you.

Whenever you think life's on top
And you don't have a prayer
Do not worry, I will be there
You will never be on your own
Together light the night
There will be no danger
My strength will be
With you forever
Feeling of eternal love
Be always in your heart
Feel the glow
It has to give be strong
With your will to live
Reach out touch embrace
I will wrap around you
Like silken lace
Open your mind
Do not be afraid
Before your soul you will find
My love in all full glory
It is yours to take
My heart in kind
Past memories fade
Into the night shade
From this day on remember
When our love was made
Never to be broken
Now mine with yours
Our dream has awoken.

A voice came from the heavens
Clear your heart, clear your mind
Take a step out of the shadows
See what you will find
Not life's answers
They are there in front of you
But life in full view
Take its wonder in both hands
Look, feel where you stand
No time for sadness in past made of glass
Be strong your strength will last
I will be there with you step by step
Close your eyes the pain you will see through
No longer a stranger in the midst of your soul
Your prayers answered
Watch in wonder as they unfold.

*W*atching clouds whisper across blue skies
My mind starts to wander
The ache in my heart knows just why
Torn in two with the last goodbye
Future plans no longer there
From the start did you really care?
As I look to the heavens above
A star shines on me, filled with love
Look around see what you have
Feel your strength move forward
Be brave, thank the angels for this day
The love that is sought is not far away
Bring not the past no tears or fear
The love that waits will soon be so clear.

*H*aving nothing to say
Eyes empty of life, lost my way
No angels playing under rainbows
No stars in midnight skies
No morning sun everything hopeless
Life going forward a void of darkness
A whisper I heard you call my name
Your kiss awoke my heart
Eyes awake your now here for me
No more dreams of darkness sadness no madness
No need to drink from life's stream of illusions
Mistakes I have made in my own confusion
Let me forgive yours too, are we not human
No longer trapped together
Wrapped in each other's love
For warmth, protection now and forever
Until eternity strikes the midnight hour
Let us begin our new direction.

*I*f my heart had wings
It would take flight
Not by day
But in the heat of the night
Hurt no more
No need to sell my soul
Await the angel's call
Listen to all you believe
But feel from your heart
Never to be alone
Hold on tight to your dreams
Do not let go
Surrender your sorrow
Feel your spirit
Lost love blessed with happiness
Let sunshine back into your life
Time will pass new dawns begin
Mistrust no longer
Take a step out look around
Find the love lost within.

My life gets stronger with every sunrise
The past more distant with every night fall
Memories just memories
No more pain scars healed
You never knew me to ask how I feel
I will not look at what could've been
Future laid out something you never seen
Wrapped up in your own little world
Time went by the more I was fooled
Your cloak of lies and deceit
Drained my love made me weak
Now I sit watch those memories fade
A smile in my heart with the life I've made
Strong am I to forgive
Have your life it is yours to live
A kiss in sympathy I blow to you
Will I ever come to your rescue?
That I doubt you made your choice
Never again will you hear my voice

ACKNOWLEDEGEMENTS

A special thank you to Lisa Wilson and Kate Saunders, without their help, and encouragement, this book would have never been created.

To all the people below who have been there for me and also complimented my work... Thank you all...

Russell & Sally Smith, Robert & Sarah Hands, Steve Woodward, Chris Dix, Ian & Julie Goldingay, Gavin & Tracy Oliver, Angela Hanlon, Angela Grant, Lisa Cole, Lisa Derby, Lisa Archer, Emma Devaney, Mandy Kowalik, Kelly Jackson, Karen Wilkins, Cherie, Dipti Morjaria, Andy Cook, Dan Owen, Fay Nicholas, Danni Kinsey, Sarah Press, Matthew White, Chloe Peters, Tia Carty, Sezzaloo, DJ, Robbo, Mags Courtney- Brown, Bill Rice, Julie Anderson, Lads in the Ivy Leaf Sports Room, Hilary Cotton,Dean Finnerty, Lynne Doak...

Last but not least yourself the reader... thank you.

Lightning Source UK Ltd.
Milton Keynes UK
UKOW04f1342281214

243644UK00001B/21/P